Coming Through Smoke
and the Dreaming

Selected
Poems

RON WELBURN

The Greenfield Review Press
Greenfield Center, New York

State of the Arts

NYSCA

Publication of this book has been made possible, in part, through a grant from the literature Program of the New York State Council on the Arts.

Published by The Greenfield Review Press, P.O. Box 308, Greenfield Center, New York 12833

ISBN 087886-144-0
Library of Congress Number: 00-134935

Publication Acknowledgments

Cover art: *A Free Woman,* by Carla Lynn Davids (Sauk & Fox/Creek)
Art photograph by Barbara Howe
Photo of author, Ron Welburn: Courtesy of *Poets of Massachussetts,* University of Massachussetts

Cover and interior design by Sans Serif, Inc., Saline, MI

Cherrie's book

Contents

From Shinnecock 40

Acknowledgments

Thanks to editors of the following journals and anthologies in which several poems in this book were published; some have undergone minor revision: *Archae2 (Fascicle 1):* A Beauty Song; *Blind Alleys:* Dee Dee, Family Circle; *California State Quarterly:* Chiaroscuro of Morning; *Callaloo:* Bones and Drums; *Community Review* (LaGuardia Community College, CUNY): A Loom of Old Songs; *The Eagle: New England's American Indian Journal:* The Blue Arrow, Holding the Courtship Drum, Shinnecock 40; *Gatherings: The En'Owkin Journal of First North American Peoples:* Festival at Shorakoppak, Masks, This Is Our Split; *Groundswell:* Mohawk Memory; *The Magazine to Re-Establish the Trickster:* Cross–Step; *North Country: An Anthology of Contemporary Writing from the Adirondacks and the Upper Hudson Valley:* Mohawk Memory, Moment of Prayer; *North of Upstate:* Photographs of Old Friends; *Pig Iron:* In the Absence of Gourds; *Returning the Gift:* Sentinel Robins; *Studies in American Indian Literatures:* Basketball and Dancing.

Thanks to Western Connecticut State University for a small AAUP grant which assisted toward the composition of some of these poems.

In the Absence
of Gourds

Family Circle

Something that happened long ago
in the face of surrender,
in the heart knowing the broken circle—
the multitudes of white leaves,
the long rifles like trees in the snow,
the mud color of chained wrists,
the heads stuck onto posts,
the bounties on those heads—

Our gestures conformed
and often the mind.
The circle lingered in a few hearts.
It must have been what wakes me
every morning with a firebrand
to go back to the Eastern Shore and
the trail leading southwest to the Blue Mountains,
to call home those families and gather them
into a pow wow as big as the secret they bear,
to talk of this long sleep
and remove delusion from the circle,
from old memories manifest
by angles of faces;
to sit in circles singing of the deer
and of bravery and the hawk;
to sit in circles singing of
big houses and council lodges.
Then, to dance, dance
round that symbolic tipi.

Self–Righteous Moment

When I was fourteen
I never feared
the Russians
the Chinese billion
the way
I distrusted
American States
the way
with my native trees removed or massacred
or mine enslaved chatteled
led me unsurprised for
3 Mile Island in Susquehannock
and that crashed carrier bomber
the Pentagon
nonchalantly decided to reveal
had missed a seventh stage for detonation
for destruction of
Cherokee country—Tsali's land.
When I was fourteen
I knew so much about
Pontiac, Chief Joseph's march,
Nat Turner, Sequoyah, Mangas, Crazy Horse—
them Russians
didn't worry me at all.

West Chester, Pennsylvania, 1914

They say
great–grandfather Gover
would leave the house
for the barn and the company
of his horses
when his wife
great-grandma Cook
on many a verbal rampage
spat fire, chestnut burrs,
and words that kept butter
hard in her mouth.

They say
He would sing
something he'd made up,
a hymn or a holler,
or some sort of
bluesy pre-49,
a lament for himself
and the treatment he got.
He didn't like to argue, you know.

Jazz

My friends across the street have a few records,
 just as do some of my relatives:
 "Take 5" is popular this summer; "Exodus"—
does that tell me something?

I am never good at this dancing,
especially under the critique one gets from the baobob soul.
How many times have I asked them to show me
the Slop and whatever else is the latest?

I like Chuck Berry, Marve Johnson, Ernie K. Doe,
and my friends can't tolerate how I can listen to
Jimmy Clanton, Dion & the Belmonts, Dwayne Eddy,
just as much as the Coasters and Shirelles.

I turn to jazz and immerse my feelings
and my thoughts in its cloak of mystery.

But that isn't simply what it's all about.

I am trying to explain to Gwen one lonely confused evening
how different I feel about something, about who I am
and what rivers have brought me here; and she tries to simplify
it all the way some people try to make a blossom out of stone
by breaking it several times.
Her sympathy is that *We* are different,
and I am aware of her "We."

I've been hearing another music out there
and don't know how to find it. What I can't seem to find
is a round dance
that turns outside of time.

Basketball and Dancing

Rejecting both as intimacies for now
I am seeking a design
for my breechclout and moccasins
and the truest leering grin for my false face.

I find several brass instruments,
bent, curved, valved, and keyed.

I go out to the world and say:
I am Young Singing Shield.
Your hoop I cover with the skins of my enemies.
Your music I convert
beyond cognizance,
for I seek this design without finding the bear
or just the right sapling
to hang his meat from.

Masks

And we too
wear a mask,
stoical, frowning,
an open-faced look
if not unforgettable;
a look that can look through you.

Under this mask
we smile and laugh and
twist our faces like
corn husks and the grains of trees.

We know, listen to
a whole lot of coyote jokes,
with and without coyote.
Whole nests of them.

We can trick you off your trails.

This Is Our Split

DuBois studied Color in Philadelphia,
and Chester County is not—
nor in the city could they be lumped as one.

Go southwest and the land rises.
Turtles once thronged there.
The people did not create the 500s, the Jack & Jills.
They visited Quogue and Montauk. Not Sag.
But yes, there is a twoness here.
The census people came and scanned us.
Shaking their heads they scribbled illiterately
on their lists and moved on,
to be followed by land thieves and bounty hunters
seeking money for new slaves.

We have strong roots, though mingled.
A longtime ancestry gives us our faces.
We came here from nowhere in particular
and from right down the road.
We are Lenapes left over; Nanticokes,
stray Piscataway families, stealthy Minquas
the Paxton Boys thought they'd wiped out.
We are shirt-wearing Tuscaroras hiding in
the Blue Mountains hearing about the Minisink.
We are asteroid Cherokees drifting around
the Susquehanna Valley and the Schuylkill.
Our names like Swannock become Swan.
Our names are Cook and Gover and Pierce.

Our names are West and Greenhill and White and Gray.
Our names are Mason, Bowers, Proctor, and Draper.
Our names are Welburn and Tyre, Shippens and Burton.

Listless in this survival,
we belong to nations we do not remember
and to people who have forgotten us.
We are the lost birds and the outcasts.
Our children never seem to know the trees,
nor have moments with the blades of grass;
the nuthatch's scolding means nothing.
Our children must be reminded
that crow is the first bird one hears in the morning.

Thus our twinness answers Dubois.
This is our story.
This is our split.

The Old Bald Man with a Secret

We carry into the battle of the day
the secret of our bones, thought upon
so seldom, and we may lose it.

Grandchildren's western war games,
war whoops, scalp 'em cavalry,
Daniel Boone, the pioneers, then the mention of
Joseph Brant awaken in the old bald man
the secret his father told him.

He looks at his children
and in their walk and in the angle of their faces
lies the secret;
in their bones, the knowledge of who they are,
lies hidden his father's lessons.
In the very impact they make then upon the world
he sees vividly his wife and his father's people.

The old man's secret finds
an oblivious world, coldly yet rolling its eyes
should he unveil.
His secret relaxes down the decades
to Jimmie Lunceford, Hi-Fidelity
and Ray Charles, until perhaps
one special grandchild remembers that
he was more than just an old bald man with a secret,
more than just one old man
whose children had lost their mother,
more than just another old man
sometimes drinking too much.

In the Absence of Gourds

In the absence of gourds,
plastic water jugs must do
for birds to drink at my yard.
Both concession and another gesture
of survival, stoking inward fires of ancestry.

I do not look the same
as I did half a millennium ago
on the threshold of invasion, then slavery;
on the eves of annihilation and disease.

None of us has exactly that look,
though we all distinctly look alike,
and have the same sounds in our speaking:
a certain round directness,
a special quill texture to our sharpness,
proud, measured, and uncluttered mouths.

Though we may speak no Indian tongue,
we hear the ghosts
of our languages
in what we say.

The Lookalike

The guy thinking you were me
had peered into my eyes asking:
"Are you Holly West?"
And what could I say?

And when I did meet you
what else could I say?
Long-lost Cherokee cousins, I suppose.
Make it a marquee sign,
"The dividing of the Wests,"
and we'll sell tickets.
I propose we start our own legacy
in this absence of mountain memory
that turned us into jazzmen
and brownskinned buckaroos.

Knowing what I know,
our faces are two top shell plates
of this Turtle island.
There is no mistake.
Arkansas or Virginia,
there simply is no mistake.

Bones and Drums

For Lewis McMillan

Generations unfold from our faces.
We have found Kwanza celebrants
and bearers of Yoruba, Ibo, and Muslim
names with connections among the Chickasaw:
a hoop broken like the faces, mouths,
a few brows native to Apalachicola, Catawba,
Creek, and the Ramapos.

Has America ever noticed
how some of these voices match
the trombone? The big horn of
"Big Chief" Russell Moore,
Fletcher's Charlie "Big" Green,
Snub Mosley,
the Jack Teagarden we speak of.
Does America recall Chief Shunatona
at the '28 Inaugural?
What does it know of Willie Colon, Steve Turre,
and so many salseros in this bull eagle's
timbre of speaking?

Have they listened to the bass,
a tree of rhythm smooth as a Jimmy Blanton,
sinewy as Oscar Pettiford, thickset as Mingus,
supple as Rick Rozie?

Or the drums; Baby Lovett to Sunny Murray,
for a basic two-step,
a round dance grass dance beat on the stretched
snare hide of Ponca City, Tishomingo, Okmulgee, Tahlequah.
The rolling piano of Muskogee.
Sock cymbals and hi-hats of seed beads, patterned and flowing
like leaves in a river
in the split rhythm accents of 4/4.

Brenda Cooksey's Song

Into East Texas my fathers made survival
their life lines.
They changed their way of seeing.

I never learned who I was.
The stories of the Bowl and the Old Settlers
I learned to ignore.

What does my face do for me
but ache ever for a mask
unsuited to its contour?

My hair wouldn't stay bush.
My cheeks flow upwards to my eyes.
I live for now,

but my heart,
born broken, seeks the escape
mundane in design.

My fathers came west from the mountains
when they could see the treachery of treaties unfold.
Arkansas, Texas, Mexico
are not my home.

Mohawk Memory

Schoharie County, N. Y.

Atop this mountain ridge I can glory in the night as
the shooting stars spear through the sky like lacrosse balls.
The Mahican are having a little fun tossing orbs from the east.
Under the dark of the moon
the Haudenasaunee must cover all goals
and can throw nothing back.

All other stars resting above us tend to their business:
the hunter, the family of sisters,
the two bears before coyote tricked them of their tails.

Above the trees to the northeast,
that Place Beyond the Openings,
a light show proceeds and heavy drums filled with water
overwhelm the sounds the winds make.
This is a distance from Skohar'le
but there is a mixture of sounds and glows
on the horizon like the redcoats and their logs
spewing fire, moving westward
to Cherry Valley.

The show is a thing of power and beauty
from where I stand,
the night but a comment, a story told in summer,
of how we once lived.

Didn't You Used to Write Stuff?

What were you writing about and
who were the people you described,
walking along roadsides and through streets and fields?
How many identities had they unknown to you?
And what did everyone call them
and what did they say of themselves?

Their memories are like yours,
pressed through a sieve except they did not entertain
what to everyone else but you
and a few others sounded outrageous.
So what! You were told.
Be what is expected of you.
Be what *they* think you are.

You knew of Little Turtle,
Cornplanter, Red Jacket, and Logan
before you learned another language.
The Lenape tongue, written down,
meant a whole lot of good things for you.
You learned bits of tracking,
differences of design,
to know what was yours.

Then a crowd of house sparrows and starlings
succeeded in taking over your affairs;
and what you wrote about was a meeting place
of the gothic and the idea of the kente cloth.
You had good style but those birds simply wanted you
to "get down!"

19

Thank Tecumseh's brother and Handsome Lake,
and thank Dragging Canoe and old Teedyuskung
for sitting aboard your shoulders all those years,
patient and undaunted,
never going away.

The Meeting Place

For the late Mary and Bob Atkinson

Hardened by Xit's "cement prairie" we gathered in a storefront in central Brooklyn, or at whatever arena granting four hours space. Some big houses these! Not even seven sides. A language to speak and songs to be tried out for the first time, my goodness in *lieder*! Our meeting places shift around like shadow figures on the walls of a strange cave; and in our urban longhouse we take on clan identities, then all of us play skeptic with glass beads. Drum? Power? Identity? Our hearts have overlong searched for unity. And now where are all those Cherokees whose lip service traipsed through our neighborhoods? And how are we here, stumbling, standing, walking, and for a while, very alone?

A Movie Pawnee at His Death

*The movie Dances With Wolves seems to portray
the Lakota people sympathetically as human beings.
Not so the Pawnees.*

for Ezra Fields

I guide my horse midstream into the Lakota circle,
and their closure silences me.
Every day is a good day to die,
and I am in their fist, a boy's arrow deep in my thigh.
In the mad eyes of the Lakota circle
I can see the stars, the faces of my ancestors
longer than memory; and in those burning Lakota eyes
I can see my last trail begin.
I circle my horse to them and
raising my club,
shout my last battle song.

*I am coming, elders, to join the fighters
and the star-bloodied maidens you told of.
I am coming to you, mothers, tillers of this Mother Earth.
I am farmer and warrior
tired of six white man treaties giving over
our homelands since my father's time.
Thirty Lakota rifles poise. Eyes aflame,
telling me I will lie to them no more,
nor fight them, raid them for horses, for blood no more.
I will not fear them again.
I raise my black club matted with the old enemy's blood*

and I yell my defiance, my anger,
my battle song.

Ancestors, I am a man.
Farmer and Warrior.
I have come.

Cross-Step

for Slow Turtle

They are astute in their dancing,
these sachems,
slick and tough with their cross-step.

Their jackets and pants—
out of regalia—clothe motion
wiser than themselves.

They strut, around the circle;
their hats uncocked nor sassy.

Fingers pocketed, their thumbs
lead them and their feet,
shod in a heel or soft leather
cross the drum beat front and rear.

This is evening when we all dance
and sit along the path the sun
always etches for us,
visiting, dancing, telling stories.

We sing, too,
and admire our old men
who have known foreign wars
and jukeboxes,
and keep up the good fight
for home.

Festival at Shorakappok

Inwood Park, Upper Manhattan
14 September 1991

We arrived at Shorakappok, the Sitting-Down place, ready to stand, and its spirits helped us through this long day. This is a village again, Shorakappok, for a special time. Singers beat the drum, stories come alive, and electric music too makes an offering as we work. Feel the ancestors' strengths this day; their touch is vocal and sensate. They live here amidst burial places for their men and women and dogs and the sturgeon. They are strong here, speaking from white willows of the clouds and the river's edge, their whispers curling like sycamore bark. The emissary bees persist to tell of this village sticking into the river like a poised egret's neck. Across the bay that white-plumed fisher studies the shallows all afternoon, alert and still, teaching a patience we've lost too soon. Gulls too play here, drifting above crowds, casually turning their heads left and right. Perhaps they know the caves where the Reckawawanc's people concealed themselves from the Mohawks only to flee down island to Dutch perfidy; caves filled with shells we covered our dead with for a while. Lost places still here, closed at *N'ashaue-kuppi-ok*, the Closed-Between Place, closing sycamore around us here as we stand, trading ironies like the exchange for Manhattan. The spirits of this place listen and whisper and some of us know how standing amidst a crowd is for listening, then stepping aside to feel their breath in the leaves.

25

A Language for Time

And the days return, as each morning
gathers up the light and sets it,
often in the colors of flame,
cooling fires banked off somewhere
at the ridged hills preparing for evening.
As crows, then doves and robin
mark the sunrise, the invisible peepers
begin serenading the twilight.

These lives and hosts of other signatures
reveal what the hours impose on us,
giving conditions to trinket us away
from land and pure water and
the people who live all around us.
Hours, minutes, the day of the week
give forth a duplicitous concept of time.

We still haven't adapted, fully.
We enjoy, as she once said,
"a bad case of Indian time,"
and all darker brothers are in league with us.
What valor and what love is knowing
where to be the precise hour of the day?
We hear our news at 5;
our music at 6:30;
we go to the toilet at 2 . . .

The body sets its pace and we wait
for its signals, listening to drum beats and

heeding the fevers.
When the runners go to villages far away,
telling the leaders to attend council
to talk about you, take a book to read:
a Momaday or a Joyce, something by Dorothy Richardson
or Silko or Morrison, Cortazar; something to prepare you
to listen to the elders and the children.
Come to know and learn
how their pace sets their words.

Other Earth Design

The fur trade brought for the crows
more than they would usually eat
and now the automobile and
the eighteen-wheeler make crow food,
and the gulls have joined the meal.
Tumulting chaos on land with
unfishable seas brings forth
these black and white weavings.
I watched their designs along roadways,
these aggresive porcupine quills,
swooping, floating, reconnoitering,
dancing and strafing each other over kills
and McDonald throwaways.
What a design they made that day,
desperate and wonderful
on the asphalt-covered breast of Mother Earth.

The Moment of Prayer

While not forest bred
I know the trees as more than foliage.
I believe in the power and the glory of the sun
and have never felt the same about prayer
seated or kneeling, my hands clasped,
in a brick structure serene with lovely glass
as I do amidst ash and birch and pine.
Perhaps it was that hill rising
behind the house where I lived,
a hill my short legs ventured to climb
that seemed so far, so upward and eternal,
its floor carpeted with the oldest leaves.
Knowing this begins the moment of prayer
that takes us through our lives
to our longest journey.
My grandfather lives in the sun
the greatest of stars
the oldest of ancestors whoever I am.
Yes, I have sat in storefront churches
and in cathedrals, and have prayed in my home,
kneeling or standing,
and I know there is no prayer
as full as that which can brush the sky
and the leaves of grass, and the moss.
Sitting across a fallen timber beneath
redstarts and sentinel jays,
I attain the strength of peace, and then

. know my grandfather's knowing
as I stand tall before him,
my feet in the earth's hair,
my arms raised high with the trees.

To Dream
of Summer

Young Writer

Oh, he was writing then!
Focusing! Cooking with gas!
And images stood him up
in his sleep and got him out of bed
to chase them down
the way he'd pursued dates
who'd gone off with other guys.

Cigarettes dangled from his lips,
ashes poised above
the old iron Smith's perforating spool.
Loneliness was a stranger then.
Monk's melodies enveloped the work room.
Somebody'd brought over Sonny Rollins's *Worktime*
or *Steamin' with Miles*.
The writer's life!

Essays emerged and editorials;
reviews of a book or an album.
The kindred never thought of money but of the word.
He even offered poesies on fingers to love
about young girls local and visiting and furry.
Lots of them.
Holding his arm, a few, or like most,
making tracks in his slumber.
Seeing the Muse,
never knowing her name.

Time of Departure

(June 1967)

Adulthood came
as multiple shifting rhythms
        slower personal
shadows evening presses away

        (Two have spawned
seeds to their prosperity
        (Two have spun
gossamer in the spiraling halls
        of the wind/ we
have shed our youthful loves
        like a heavy cloak)

        I have observed myself
like a winter starling among us,
no footnoted passions in my notes.
Now she carries her unsown grain
to a distant sunrise; and I,
to the night, words for
another instinctive song.

Dee Dee

The walking sandpiper
bobs its tail up and down
like a girl I knew named

snipes.

Her walk wasn't quick or jerky
but a smooth rhythm
between a stroll and a slow dance.

She even resembled a sandpiper—
had an overbite her warm color
had me excuse.

You had to have seen it to believe.

The Man Next Door

Clinton Avenue, Albany, N. Y.

the man next door

is a young man

with a young wife

and a young son

and a young dog.

I do not know

how he speaks to his wife, but

he shouts at his dog and

he shouts at his son.

It is always the same.

Some Kind of Indian

Leaving the party I walk you through
the Caribbean streets to your door.
You're about as foreign to this country
as black corn.
"I hear you're some kind of Indian"
you say, and do I guffaw
against the light wind and
the unusual stillness.

Yes, I'm something, alright, and even
while striding with you I'm sitting on a fence
kind of charmed by dancing with you
and with reading the shy smile in your quiet laughter.
"Chickasaw" you say you have.
And I seem to have so many the best I can make of it all
is turtles and flowered moccasins.

I'm not trying to convince you,
talking a good line.
There are just some things
I've always known; like,
I'm a little bit kinky, too.

When Turtle Looks for Women

There is always fresh dirt in my face
and dust to clog my eyes and throat.
I suppose then I should feel
fortunate I have a half-dozen women
to call,
to chat with,
to go with for a sandwich or fish,
attend an exhibit
or a pow wow,
or simply
just ride around the long dry roads of
acquaintanceship.

I have a soft ear
and will listen to them.
One calls me her guide
announced by a seer.
Another appreciates my patience, perhaps,
or some inborn way
I seek peace with myself.

I feel like an 1800s man,
a hunter revisiting in the space age
to settle a score or reach an accord with the Twins.
Unlike Joe Bataan,
all my *Gypsy Women* play with fire;
all my *Special Girls* can't stand blue.

For years I've wondered what my problem is.
Bad breath? Underarm?
Or am I the sucker no lady has time for?
Some rusty saddle tramp I am.
When I ride into town
even the sleaziest whores
turn in their linen.

To Dream of Summer

Summer, and the dreams of summer
will soon be through; the dreams of
ballgames and outdoor music
attended by women in backless blouses
and women whose breasts hold up haltertops.
The dreams of summer making the succession
of slow days gallop into the first frost, and
toward the even lengths of night
above the canopies of yellow trees.

Summer, and a time for dreaming,
of the soft-skirted women in sandals and espedrills
and platform corks,
of the fussily dressed clean-toed women
vaunted in wedgies and resting their hips
in the wire-bottomed chairs of outdoor cafe's.

To dream of summer
when snow and the gray sun covers all this surface,
when boots turning smartly at the ankle yield
glamour and bosoms are downed against velour.

To dream again of summer in springtime,
to anticipate the culottes and the slave slippers,
the curbside hotdogs and diet soft drinks.
Babaganoush and the curious yankee ladies
buzzing before it, encouraged by
their worldly sisters
to dream of summer
in the cool wet evenings of May.

Young Mister Redwing

Young Mister Redwing's got

this shaft of brown weed

in his beak. It's thick and

it'll reenforce the nest like a twig.

He's so young the yellow

on his wings

has yet to come in.

There's a gleam in his eyes

and you couldn't tell him *nothin'*.

It's his first love.

Raven, Killer Whale, Crow

The hunters, muscled
into masked longboats,
rowed on to where the wounded,
deadly lances now in their backs,
thrash to crack open the boats
and kill men with their tails.

Her fathers the ravens
join his ancestor crows to sing,
to dance this cetaceous venture.
How simply painted he is,
looking upon her gorgeous designs,
the evening rainbows of her beak
accepting the fruit he offers,
her soft eyes intense and yielding.

Raven, Killer Whale, Crow.
The gulls that unite them
with the sinew of their wingtips
have strayed to the Smoking Mountains, and
at the magic lake they are forbidden to see
have witnessed the great wounded bear
who sings legends of sea beings.

For her, memory
of hunting at sea
rises to the story and song and
to the fixed necessity of this love.

Raven, Killer Whale, Crow.
Their stories endow purpose to the gulls
to fly before messenger winds
to rise dancing and singing,
as whales breaching signatures
on the turquoise sea.

In Autumn Serenade

*(Recommended reading while listening to
"Autumn Serenade" performed by Johnny
Hartman and John Coltrane, recorded for*

Impulse Records in 1963)

In "Autumn Serenade" the voices coast through the air crisp of October, warm in some memory of the kiss and the soft squeezing hand. The lines from the reed possess notes that are full, each having distinct weight like something solid that is malleable. At an instant a note or an arabesque glissandi seems to split open its sound and reveals something like a yolk or a hum of the trees or some other live thing; a split open sound always October in the overtone each note lives by, as things living hold on to their milieu's connective tissue. At an instant an arabesque crescendo swirls the leaves beneath the knitted brow of twilight, and we wander into October, wandering by chance itself looking for memory of the kiss and the stars woven into disapproachment and illusion, and wandering an arabesque autumn twilight to the low ground in the dark courtesies of harmonique. The saxophone makes new all those Octobers, notes from its brassy body sanguine artifacts, glowing pearls of morning frost softened into melody.

Blues of the Common Man

Adamantly, we risk fortunes
of ennui searching in a mall,
growing like melons on couches,
or sitting the figment of the Goodlife.

I would say I would sing
I would dare I would dance
feverishly in springtime
amid these hills where it seems
I could spend my last dollar
on the rent like the first
and show nothing for my labor
but the county's receipt,
like a good ole boy blaming
supplementary madness on reality.

And so the Green, should I let it
be my prison and I its model inmate,
allows the security of a playing field,
just slightly sloped at one end, with
monuments of ships' bells and
the deads' long look
as I pick through this song.

An Orchestra

What does it take now
to fill the afternoons and evenings
with grainy viscera of
the saxophone sections from
orchestras of old?

Why can't we
surround ourselves again with
lugubrious bass clarinets
singing ironies
like toads awaiting
our feeble voices.

Let's have Baritones! Baritones!!
Clean articulations in Pepper Adams
and Sahib Shihab and mellow Gerry
and that "in the beginning . . ." voice
of Harry Carney and God.
Blueitt blistered the ceilings at Jabberwocky
and Carnegie Hall—
but sometimes Ronnie Cuber and Kenny Rogers
and Cecil Payne and Mario Rivera and John Surman
and the articulation proceeds
in the fashion others pepperly
lean into their solos.

All the music of mornings
lived in grand pianos
and anchored us to sunlight and rain.
We breathed mists through its strings;
hammers and pedals invoked the dew.
All we had to know how to do
was touch and be touched.

How did these orchestras
survive so long, visited sporadically
by the french horn and the dismissed tuba?
Was the voice in F an enigma here?
Duke saved his hands
to play the players to play their horns
to play the sounds
changing in his mind.
"Play it like it's your last time to play!"
And so we did when even
the literal bullet would come
in the irony of Lee Morgan's dying.

Where are the laughing
bass clarinets and
the basset horns of Pelikan's
backstage mirror image?
Where is the rest
of the orchestra?

Peresina

(After a composition by McCoy Tyner)

Peresina is the spectral ivory glare in the soft hues,
the stately undulating blue dancer of an exotic landscape.
She assimilates rainbows and sullen afternoons, dawns
at autumn and parties beginning at midnight where rhythm
and horns of brass and cane can ritualize her.

Peresina wears velours to be concealed by forests,
lavender pants and thigh-high suede boots for those
crepescular encounters of inviolate heat and gibbous
laughter. Her whims are at the merciless extremes of
guilt and curiosity and she has waltzed the perimeters
of treachery and disease as mere and casual sorties
from houses abiding loneliness.

She survives through metal and music, this Peresina,
hanging on through the snag of voices beckoning silky
closures of disbelief, surviving this Peresina down
the lines legato saxophones mark with strutting asides.

She is interlude, this whimsical Peresina, with low
arabesques to feign for depression. The trumpet sound
aglare outside the tenor is the grill of expensive automobiles
arriving, long imaginary Cinderella metals heady in
pursuit of gleaming flights, geese forgotten in the
November skies, alto saxophones calling Peresina
to miscue so many suave voices.

Sketches of Spain: The Jacket

What they call nostalgia
is actually a treatment of
the memory of touch or of the smell of
strawberries, or the way an album cover
appeared in shadow
while you listened to the music.

Sketches of Spain.

I held the burnished yellow
and russet cover with the question-mark figure
—his signature—toreadored,
in my hands and it was not frayed
at the edges the way Bernard's was, and
my evening this early autumn of '91 was
nothing like that youthful winter
I first heard Miles, on record.
Perhaps even the music was not the same
though melody spoke tentatively in harmon voice,
and despite the Gil Evans fanfare for "Saeta,"
and the buoyantly gallant trance of "Solea."

So much of the horn remains.
Yet even if this album cover frays into
dog-eared glory, my evenings will conflict;
and with Miles gone I will always have
two memories early and late.
I will have such great music without the smell
vinyl leaves in a young man's nose,
without the dim livingrooms edged by diningroom chandeliers.

The sound once lived in those places.

I would listen then; I would flamenco.
I can step to the intertribal
in this my freer mood,
and it is all
memory's stuff and all phases of Gil and Miles
and all the phases of being a man.

Nostalgia is neither bitter nor sweet,
but glory in the smell
of one's music coming of age.

Madge
1906–1989

"Of Quogue, East Quogue, and Thereabouts"

I met you at Shinnecock, down the road
from Quogue, one day recalling
an afternoon in my livingroom,
and me a small boy
greeting an orange-hued
Cousin Clarence Greenhill,
a man with my mother's name and mine
and her mother, Viola West, on a window shade
that rolled up almost two centuries, maybe more,
of a Cherokee family and others.
And then, off I was sent to play.

And east of Quogue and thereabouts,
I am always in our cramped livingroom,
I can always raise my arms to the sun
and sing the old words that boy tried to teach me.

As you sat behind your necklaces,
I knew you as the one whose calm and snap
together anchored me to that livingroom,
more dear than an oyster pearl,
and profound as a whale beached from the sea.

Photographs of Old Friends

(Crazy Horse, and daughter)*
Montclair, New Jersey, April 1984

There is a room in one's home
where you the visitor can retreat.
Where you for whom and with whom
the host breaks bread can rest your bones
at night, or in the afternoons
when there is no need for brooding
or sharing a moment in your stay.

Rest, and be welcome,
for old friends of the home
smooth away your doubts
from their soft textured placement
along the walls;
old friends heavy in their hair and eyelids,
blanketed and speaking a secret dialect,
smiling a confidence or displaying
what seems to the world like a frown;
watchful and listening
to the spirit you bring
to a guest room—their room—
and the peace they give to this home,
a tree in which they too rest velvety as doves.

Sentinel Robins

From the trees at the Shinnecock homes
young robins scout the roads,
ready for dog soldier days,
ready for intruders and outside related
daring to sack the Rez.

The robins keep me in sight
on a morning walk to take in
the cove and the salted air.

Silently they edge just ahead of me,
tree to bush, tree to obscured fence post;
males young and tough and still
vaguely spotted.
Nesting is over
and they have come into seasoning
for stalwart duties older than memory.

These days strife still comes along
before, as in the old times,
a village could prepare for it.
Blood spills and war clubs
of the hand and mind raise;
legs broken.

Going onto the Rez late one night
I heard sentinel robins
call out their resonant warning.
But we're here to celebrate

Labor day's 39th, hoping
there'll be a 49th Pow Wow
and maybe a good-time 49.
We're redwing brothers
who've come in peace many times
to share in the fun and
be with our friends.
No one's looking for an ugly afternoon.

Shinnecock Arms

Long memory finds your Grand-Mamá
up in the widow's walk of her house
looking seaward many an afternoon,
awaiting the Circassian's return.

In this mansion here at Quogue,
red fisherman families live; and here
the child that you were
climbed the lofty stairwell
to glimpse an oft-told light and
savor the smell of fish
mingled with the salted deck.

The child you were mounted
in the footfall of your Grand-Mamá's
echoing steps—
        Atop this white crow's nest
you stand face to face with Sugarloaf Mountain
as the ocean's feathers
spread out at your back—
        There was
an evening the storm arose like
an angry god; the Enoses and Lees kept vigil,
the wind rending their patient nerves and
twisting their boatload of sons,
wringing out cargo onto requiem's shore.

You come down from that observatory
of your house, a child filled
with legacy, dreaming the wonder
shaped and beaded from disaster.

Now this mansion, called Shinnecock Arms
since you left your bedroom,
sits in silence,
its façade rent by neglect
its white paint dulled to the color
the fog wore in that night long
before your birth yet ever on your tongue.
And in the morning
when tears flowed into your beached uncles,
flowing as they do now,
in a muffled sob,
sitting before this place of watching,
your heart
in your home's compassion,
can see all this great expanse of time.

That Look of Yours

They have accused you
of looking right into
a person, right into
their souls,
right straight
through the flesh and their bones
reading evasions deeper
than secrecy and the passion
for deceiving.

They must fear you.
They must know you can see under water.
Already you know this:
how surfaces of lakes and oceans and reservoirs
hide schools of tiny fish following the leader,
schools of human beings swimming
in circles,
afraid to look through the water
as you do,
at this vast small-minded world.

The Long View

We travel this land and wonder
and see and listen til we can't stand ourselves
anymore—
that's a way to live!—
And we can't stand ourselves
going home again—that too!—
In this long view all of home.

But what is home to us?
We aren't dog inclined to drop down
to gather others' fleas;
nothing irresponsible to manhood;
no places off limits.

Home becomes the empathy and assimilation
of the paths of travel,
following this millennial dust and thickets
cleaved by parties of war and the hunt.
Envoys to distant nations and to
whole peoples suffering dislocations.
Earth-mothered peoples like ourselves.

"The Indian loves to wander," you've said.
This continent is our home—that inch
the sign in your guest room proclaims taken 3000 miles.
We embrace special valleys and hillsides,
long mesas looking from afar
like turbans upon the earth, and mountains
where hawks astride bears
take our breath away.

We chew on and salivate those memories,
this walking this driving long miles
to meet our friends.
Alive we are stuffed into cities and suburbs
like swallows into gourds the same way
we pack the highways through summers;
and we rise like prayer smoke
to the faces curious of our living.

Looking ahead. The long view
trained us for traffic, forward across
the burning roads and remembrances.
Tree-studded hills offered their challenge.
I climbed as much of a hill I could
behind the house I lived in.
Brown leaves cascaded through my ankles
and a smell of dampness and bark
remains on my hands.

I know the seeing distance, looking
forward and peripherally the roads.
You know me enough to notice
what I miss sometimes close at hand!
From my hills of home,
I looked out as the goldfinch flies over
gulleys and scrub edgeways,
beyond power lines and the railroad,
out a journey my young legs marveled at walking
the long view so easy to touch and smell.

This is yours and mine,
this Long View
making our souls its home.

Scudded Sky Evening

Sea fishermen's blood
courses her veins,
pumping that strong heart that knows how
scudded skies will
soak tomorrow longer than the dew.

Beauty alone designs this sunset.
The water above us roams muted
in gold and orange and odd wonderful
shades of lavender and blue.

Scallop clouds.
Shell row upon shell row.
She knows them.
We see her make with them
a mantle of heaven to wear
dancing, stomp dancing
around the fire that evening.
Scallop clouds,
clouds with secret colors,
shells in hands
held beneath the mantle of the evening.

Never deny this design
or doubt the heart whose ancestry,
lost in the storm off Quogue,
moves on the water
intimate with the gale winds.

The Grandfather Corn

Each day of those later pow wows she lifted the grandfather corn from her glass case and, breaking off a kernel, gave a piece of her ancestry to the open hands of a child. She knew she was completing a circle, and as often as she felt the weight of the blessing bestowed in giving, the blessing and its domain overwhelmed her.

The words *sacred* or *frightened* were spoken but that wasn't it. She gave freely the kernels she twisted from the hull of dried pale sustenance in honor of the stones whose bodies she adorned with beads and bone and shell and wire. Silver is a soft metal, and corn is soft and each piece taken will give a child a night of rest in this world's restless tumult.

Each piece given is a story of the *samp* eaten in Quogue and memories of Sugarloaf Mountain.

Each piece given is a story of walking back to Rome, Georgia all the way from Tahlequah on a path marked by tears.

With each kernel of this white corn she gave something of legacy, the proud inevitable return.

Inwood Park, Manhattan

I could feel something there
that afternoon.
Something definite, unplaintive,
alone and watchful.

Several whispers mingled with us,
or perhaps it was her,
or something of the day
that brought out Reckawawanc villagers
from Harlem to meet their upriver sachems.

Ones stronger than flesh
and perhaps her among them too,
for she once sighed and laughed
over the water and talked there
among her beads and silvered stones.

And I knew it and felt it in me,
touched by what the still air
made of that presence.

From Shinnecock 40

Shinnecock 40

We arrange in circles
to dance and to trade,
some of us for a time
whose first flight is long forgotten.

The sun infects us with joy
and makes well our ailments,
wiping tensions from our brows.

Whatever the Red Tail Singers
drum—their honoring songs,
grass dance songs, two-steps—
braids their voices with
the Youngbloods and
the Thunderbirds.

Brothers, Sisters
unseen for months,
flock here like geese
to a favorite place.
The drums braid us together
and the songs paint new colors
in regalia.
Everyone walks in beauty these afternoons.
We can feed ourselves a little longer now.
The sun and the drums and our Maker
lift our spirit like a flock
veeing towards heaven.

Holding the Courtship Drum

Courting like a ruffed grouse
a man has to concentrate,
be oblivious to vehicle drone.
You're at the edge of trees.
You fan and strut into display
with your chest poked out,
your neck swollen to get down.
The woman you've got a bead on
is in a thicket, pretending
to ignore you; pretending
the traffic has drowned out
the sound of your drum.
She's half delighted and
she's half scared to death,
'cause in this world
if a horn's sound startles you
and breaks the drum beat,
her heart will sink into her belly
until you compose yourself again,
and lift her sweetly
to dance with you.

Somethin' Special

I've thought about that somethin' special,
and avoiding its intoxication and dream,
I keep to the hunter's stirrings and quest.
I rely on instincts
awaiting our moments and places
and the best we can give.

Your affection may seem like
my prey but it isn't.
Here's no pursuit of love.
After all, one of my heroes,
a hunter too,
wound up wandering the heavens
over a lady.
So, laughter of the spheres
is my lesson.

Here on the ground
my arms cup your waist.
Your hair adds lustre to my eyes.
Your fragrance lifts me from my malaise.
Bull horns embrace you:
come back this evening to their caress;
come back where our knowing awaits.

Eye-Level Love

He arrives for her
late one mild autumn night,
and they fill the moments
walking, speaking low, growing closer,
arms locked the way limbs
of two trees embrace in the nearby woods.

Lovers need this stroll
to let down the anxious wait,
to speak with hands around waists.
Lovers need that eye-level love
like looking from the side of a mountain
at an old pumpkin moon.

He made a trail through
the high country to be with her,
his heart on the horizon
beckoned, summoned to her valley
where a soft fire
would lay before him,
where she kissed his chest in her sleep.

A Loom of Old Songs

My love for her
is tied up in old songs
we remember and sang and danced as
we heard each other's voices in the night.

We could not then touch fingers.
The cities lay thick with fog;
the twilight deceived us of love.

We wandered far
seeking that thing in another
to make whole our circles,
and the majority claimed us and
directed our eyes.

We can sing today. We can dance. We are harmonies
after dark away from the sacred fire,
lost in our own 49.

In the sun, songs of urban reference
braid our fingers and give us 'Skins
that special east coast get-down.

We love drum songs.
We rattle and shawl dance
and the wise Earth Mother
keeps singing for us,
pulling us together, slowly along
the loom of our lives,

a blanket of doo-wop songs she made
of Motown soul men,
one of the looms of our lives;
a blanket of singing she made us,
a blanket full of memories of
sun faces and squash blossom eyes;

a blanket made on this loom of our life,
heavy for those long years,
for those cold nights and the path our going.

A Gift

In the pulse of the drum
and the circle, I saw your smiling
half-profile, your braids
wrapped in ermineskin.
Your dress was the morning sky
holding fast the drenched trees
next to the foaming sea.
Subtle beads trimmed you,
all white-fringed for shawl dancing
and for moments of scrubbing.
I cannot explain my whimsy to patience
in knowing your pride.
Your figure still is gift
to your lover,
his woman, serene,
your man.

Untitled Love Poem

Turning her head to wave to him,
she is the distance a birch
would lay among the trees standing
near a clearing.

Close to the trunk she smiles
into its high limbs,
branches surrounding his face,
small singing birds in his eyes.

"The Blue Arrow"

Wooing you,
I would bring fruits
and ground provision, blankets
and moccasins, laying them
at the door of your lodge.
Then a horse I'd bring for you,
a paint with black and chestnut circles.
I would then have awaited
your acceptance, the horse to ride upon,
the moccasins to live in with me,
the home to share.

My heart has not changed nor my love.
Time has, and so now
I give you this old reliable
heap of an automobile, Japanese made,
good engine, leaky body
on the verge of who knows what.
It will help you for a while—
has never let me down.
And beyond its life
neither will you.

First Dance

Our hold falls into place,
and falls to an exact contour,
our bodies pressed together
like rose petals clutching
the leaves of a closed book.
The exact contour of music
makes steamy heads
and we rise
one in motion,
locked in a slow dance:
locked together in song.

Chiaroscuro of Morning

In the chiaroscuro of morning,
the light on your bare shoulders
and back absorbs all the shadows
and pulls away from gray,
though shadows ever persist
to feed the softness of your skin.

Pine embers bank beneath your flesh,
and the morning's pastel
urges warm echoes of touch
from my hands of bronze and copper,
our pine-needle bed of embrace.

The occasions I had tended fire
somewhere in this world
getting ready to hold you
that one afternoon of singing
and the drum, readying my hands
for your shoulders, my hands
for your muted dawn skin
in our ringing songs of red.

The Beaches

Summer nights now
they have closed the beaches.
Without a private party destiny
we must escape to the city
and watch the lights high up
in buildings phase out stars and
the gibbous indiscretions of the moon.

Young gulls that slip through the night,
dark eyes gleaming star-bursts and
bellies filled with fish know
the Protectors have closed down the world,
that you and I who desire
the cooled sand around our feet
are shuttled back to the hard streets
and the coarse laughter of the lost.

We can come back here perhaps
when winter arrives to polish
the bowl of the sky in crisp lustre.
You can come here alone no more it seems,
to pull through pain and attitudes
bombarding sensibility, for the sea
teems with beauty and peace for you
and they have closed down the beaches
and the world as surely as
young laughing gulls slip
stealthily through the night.

We wander the paved perimeters,
trying to look out to the sea.
We will have no night life
combing the grasses for that path
to tranquility.
Aimlessly we wander, cynical,
as gulls young and agile and wise
slip easily through our fingers.

Let's Awake Early Feeling Strong

I awaken early, and don't recall ever
at dawn "feeling sad like so many of us do."
Senses quicken dream time and prayer:
sunlight and moon
snowbird and snow.
No slave to java,
I am charged by the smell of mornings,
by spruce and cedar leaves
opulent or brown,
by blue jay's sassy cackle,
shamed melody of the furtive thrush;
footsteps on a street;
trombones on the morning road.

Let's awaken to heroes
their peoples honor, needs
shunning self-emolition.

Storied doorway singers died on vomit
and southern comfort in bathtubs
of their lost worlds, eaten by their victims:
mescaline, scag, hashish;
audiovisual aids for the contact starved
who know the face of the tower.
What myths did Rimbaud slay?
Charlie Parker? Janis? Jim Dunn in his dilemma?
Or your latest local angry man,
dead in a bottle, veins, sinusitis
embracing Sister Salvation?

Let's awaken early to endless songs
to know the visions in everlasting dance.
The echoes of full circle dancing say
we clavé and stomp to our tribal doors,
to our inner strength and visions.
World around us, we have shunned
the populous highs:
the ganga, cocoa seeds, poppies in profusion,
the agronomics of empire,
colonial entrapment.

Let's awaken early feeling strong.

Rivers of Wind

A painting by Bill Rabbit

Each black strand,
long and thick around her face
and shoulders, flows beyond monoliths
as if pulled like the panels
of her blue-white gown.
This is a Pueblo woman before stone pillars,
large clay pots dark at her feet.
Something of the wind affects her
as she stands unplussed like those stones.
Something of the wind challenges her spirit
but her unbent resolve is fastened to
this place of faith and wisdom and the home.

She stands ready to sing.
In these rivers of wind carrying
trouble and love
she is ready to sing
to make the powers work for her life.
This last summer moon before equinox
she knows these rivers will blow around her
and swirl inward lights and rainbows.
She stands with you now
profound in your knowing,
like our elder's face and eyes
renewed to us in the moon of her birth
within the circled time of her leaving.
These are rivers she stands amidst,
her back to the wind, facing

cusps of day and night
standing to sing for you
standing to sing with you
and to the powers of the inner light.

The White Dress

Her coat is
brighter than emerald
in her man's idea;
in the eyes of
the man that are green;
in love already
with red shoes.
She is striding through
green corridors of envy,
over the runner's calves,
this woman mantled like
a shimmering meadow surrounding a cloud
where good years ascend lonely,
their dihedrals clumsy
in the updrafts,
disturbed by her coat
more than emerald
in her lover's eyes
on her scarlet high heels
with the silver hearts,
singing, singing,
singing love.

A Sentimental Reason

A gull flies near this building,

circling it sometimes, flapping away

the swift currents this far up

the penthouse, or diving into them.

One sees in the glint of its eye

how in the spark of its flight

there lies some sentimental reason,

bouyed perhaps by a crooner's songs

and the clearing skies, and

the crows playing the width

of the river like a guitar.

The Monolith

The clouds of Boston didn't stop me. The breeze rattled the windows and I fell asleep to the sibilant lull of traffic and sounds I presumed the Charles River should make. I've gone through the astrology books reaffirming your love style, and closed that part of the evening with a story, Shirley Jackson no less, familiarly arcane to not bring restless slumber. When you enter the room and undress, all my senses awaken to point out how the closed shade blocks out the hammock of sky; and when you lay down my arms and legs cradle you and the risk of detection spirits our throbbing embrace. With morning we discover outside that white sandstone architecture with tinted glass, a monolith hovering crudely around the idea I had of the red clouded sky.

Mules in Circles of Light

As they stand, backs to me,

the brass-encased spikes make circles

on the bare floor. Perfect forms

this reflected light, beneath

black soles sloping to full mane.

The circles of brass insist upon

the deep walnut stain of the floor

a balance of sunshine and siena.

Particles of dust like those I watched

a thousand years ago offer the heels

this ancient dance, and I am singing,

my vision now a burnished articulated melody.

The Fields Aromatic

The breezeless trees and the fields aromatic in the bright
mornings bouy the spirit of how lovely the colors of desire
smell and how fragrant is the idea of peace held in the hearts
of light. No greed and no job blues; no Ming's "no private
income" dues.

The trees and the fields aromatic there in front of
the mild breeze's projected smells of desire—how
lovely the fragrant notion of peace held in the hearts
of light and the turbulent shadows of intention.

The still flowers of trees and the fields aromatically
fuchsia and thistled and smiling beneath the red-wings
bouy the spirit mist of dawning slopes and the close
fragrance of strawberries and wet honeysuckle and
the inevitable return.

Beaver

Housatonic River,
New Milford, Connecticut

The surface

of the river's edge

bends around the dark

shape of the beaver

invisible to us above him,

a soft movement

in the night

large, waterproof,

leisurely swimming upcurrent

unplussed by

the rush of the cars.

Bottom at the River

Steep Rock Preserve,
Washington Depot, Connecticut

The river is loudest where it flows to.
The sound comes from that bottom mile
of our ears, sound summing to the bottom
of the line and silent at the top
as the eyes behind the brush and trees
could see, silently gathering sound
to rush downriver to the laughter
and calling the water makes back to us,
silent to the wakers downriver hearing
another bottom of the river's flow
in a waving line like a bonepipe
necklace in the fingers of prayer.

Its Anxious Moments

The moods of winter's new moon
alter the sensitivities of flesh and steel.
Sickness travels many miles
and before the first hard snowfall
it settles into our anxieties
to make us dumb.

We kiss the sun through
gray cracked trees bereft
of cardinal bloodstains
and the white cheeks of chickadees.
With our windows shut
we cannot hear the horses
at the little farm down the street
whose neighs always seem
carried by the dew.

With this bleak moon
at decade's end
the old Ford plagues us yet again.
We bed down beneath quilts and
dark walls wondering of its
annual ritual: guessing to start
in the morning or playing someone's fool
(and will be good to us if we coax and talk
to it? Will the slate cold nights atrophy
its entrails?)

Beast that it is, it too
lives in anxious moments,
ridden by the misty ghosts of autumn
the way our breath dances on the wind.

This Is for You, Miss Anne

I think the cat
envies our shiny things,
sterling spoons or silver earrings
disappear and the face is inscrutable
to our queries: she's preening
the hind foot—"Sorry we interrupted you"—
or marking a door and our bewildered stance.

We found a cache of forks
at our old place, hidden in
the back room behind a book
fallen from a table shelf.
The teaspoons . . . ?
We see salivation in
clandestine candor blinking at them
from the dining room chair.
A studious scheming, this scrutiny, and
a coy nonchalance at the sound of warning.

She doesn't care.
None of them care!
Returning home we find one bear claw
earring from our room's night stand
on the wood of my son's floor.
Hockey, you need only one puck.
The second is insurance, you see,
for those weekends she feels
insulted and bored.

Her and the Shawl Dancer (Irene)

Mashantucket Pequot: Schemitzun '92

I tell the Cree dancer how
in her shawl waiting
to fancy dance that the lights and
her glasses and certain profiles
give her resemblance to my wife
who once shawl-danced
who is embarrassed approaching
apologetically and Anishenabeg
and feigns salty in their talk
when the Cree dancer takes my arm
to run away with her
and I chuckle as if I've stepped in it now
feeling how the two lives echo
of old work and affections and
how they know what it means
to get away from the memories
for a while because the high kicks of
their fancy shawl dancing really say
how much they've already lived it.

Walking to the Moon

October 24, 1996

Off Paumanouk's south shore
three humpbacked clouds
follow me to the moon,
and they are outpacing my leisure
to walk this Amagansett beach
with no purpose but the moment.

Without you I won't indulge
the tides to lick my feet,
something about being alone here
at dusk while absorbed in the moonlight
and the white sand.

I am walking to the moon
as the sun goes down on this good day.
To the south which the clouds arch over,
my Accomac must think of this
as a small magic,
a vision of men and sea animals,
parallel travelers toward
the claw tip of Turtle Continent.

With each stride I am
closer to the grandmother of light,
closer to that place
shared by dream and the sea.

She sings my approach
so I would realize what power
she and the ocean have on lovers walking arm in arm
at this rim of the turtle.

Then, on her side of a mound,
piping plovers rise from play
to escape above the surf just as we do,
revealed to the world in a furtive kiss.

Signaled is my moment of return,
having the moon smile at my back,
at peace with my longing for you.

A Beauty Song

Come

You are gifted with dreaming.

Come through

The Smoke and the fires.

Stand in the beauties of vision.

You are Gifted with dreaming.

Come

You are seeing the fire.

Come through

The smoke and the dreaming.

Stand in the moon shadows

Beside the burning sweetgrass.

Come

you are gifted with dreaming.

Answers Moving In

The answers we seek:
seclusive in high trees
and in the deep bottoms
of silted lakes, hide
from monster fish
hatched from ravenous memories:

as parentage:
one and two and more back
to the fugitive time
when nations were untethered
and dreaming put aside.

On the turtle's back
the four herbs and three sisters
teach us ancestry: we are;
picking stones from
pine needles and generations of leaves.
Burnings for prayer
and smoke rising our hearts
to say:
Not all of us live
          bound to a land of forgetting.
Not all of us live
          bound: to a present: no memory.
Not all of us
          aboard the turtle's back
fear the sharp-toothed small fish
with antennae noses

kin to the flying heads and booger men
strafing answers rising in the lake
and coming down steathily from the trees.

Answers converge slowly
singly into our souls;
even as we wonder; our loved ones:
fools or frightened, protecting us
from the deluge,
losing us to lightning and red snow moon.

We recover:
everyone kept the sister foods.
We smoked tobacco and cooked with sage;
We learned cedar pleases the Maker;
We learn tobacco and sage;
We find where the sweetest grass grows.
Pieces handed down of memory:
We are ancestors now:
learning generations.
We are ancestors now:
Moving in: today.

Glossary

This Is Our Split: In his classic study, *The Philadelphia Negro,* W. E. B. Dubois is certain to have included Indian families as part of the African American population. The "500s" and the Jack & Jills were Black upper-middle class families and their offspring many of whom were strongly of Native descent. "Sag" refers to Sag Harbor near East Hampton on Long Island, where many families from Pennsylvania and New Jersey vacationed.

When Turtle Looks for Women: Joe Bataan, Filipino-African American singer-songwriter, was a popular Latin-Soul stylist of the middle and late '60s with "Special Girl," which praised his girlfriend's loveliness when she wore blue, and a uniquely evocative version of Curtis Mayfield's "Gypsy Woman."

An Orchestra: Trumpeter Lee Morgan, a Philadelphian who was half if not more Indian, and who was an alumnus of Art Blakey's Jazz Messengers, was gunned down by his estranged wife at Slug's Saloon, a famous jazz venue in Manhattan's East Village, where he was playing. Pelikan was a street musician in lower New York of the sixties and seventies who played the basset horn. He is a Creole from Louisiana.

Photographs of Old Friends: Madge Barnes Allen firmly stated that the pair of large framed photographs on her guest room wall were of the "original Crazy Horse" and his daughter, an adolescent whose name she did not recall. Madge defied the notion widely held that the Oglala leader was never photographed. The photos, approximately 24″ x 16,″ belonged to her father, George Barnes (1867–1930), a "going-back" Cherokee born in Tahlequah, Indian Territory. He told Madge that Crazy Horse himself presented the pictures to him when he, George, was a

101

young man, meaning sometime around 1885 or later, several years after history records the leader's demise. The man depicted wore a serene and expressive smile and appeared to be in his later forties-early fifties. The love Cherrie and I had and maintain for Madge, with whom we traveled the pow wow circuit for twelve years of learning and fun, is stronger than any desire to refute her.

Shinnecock Arms: Like many coastal Native families, the Enoses were fishermen. On December 29, 1876, six Enos brothers, Poosepatuck-Shinnecock-Narragansett according to Madge, were aboard The Circassian, a vessel floundering in a terrific storm. All six lost their lives. Abram Enos, Madge's grandfather, was recently married with a child on the way, and was advised against joining the venture. When the men's bodies washed up onto the shore, the women of the family could still feel the warmth on their chests. James Truslow Adams, in *History of the Town of Southampton* (1918. Port Washington: Ira J. Friedman, Inc., 1962), never mentions them by family name, but says ten Shinnecock Indians lost their lives, "the flower of their tribe and the last of the full bloods" (247). The Enos family lived near the Quogue shoreline in a stately home from whose rooftop widow's walk, a common structure on such houses, the women of the family awaited signs of their men's return. During the twentieth century the home's new owners converted it into an inn, Shinnecock Arms.

The Grandfather Corn: A type of white corn with puckered kernels.

About the Illustrator

Carla Lynn Davids
(Sauk & Fox and Creek) studies Fine Arts at
Our Lady of the Elms College in Chicopee, Mass.
She thanks the Creator and her late father "Son" Davids
for her gifts of love and acceptance.